HOW CAN WE BUILD A
GODLY MARRIAGE?

JOEL R. AND MARY BEEKE

REFORMATION HERITAGE BOOKS
GRAND RAPIDS, MICHIGAN

Reformation Heritage Books
2965 Leonard St. NE
Grand Rapids, MI 49525
616-977-0889
orders@heritagebooks.org
www.heritagebooks.org

Printed in the United States of America
19 20 21 22 23/10 9 8 7 6 5 4 3 2

ISBN 978-1-60178-578-7
ISBN 978-1-60178-579-4 (e-pub)

For additional Reformed literature, request a free book list from Reformation Heritage Books at the above regular or e-mail address.

HOW CAN WE BUILD A
GODLY MARRIAGE?

You did it again. You criticized your spouse in front of a friend. You said something negative about him or her to your mother. Your marriage isn't what it used to be: On a scale of 1 to 10, your relationship was once a 10. Now it is a 5 at best. Mediocrity has settled in.

In many ways, you and your spouse appear to be getting along. You don't argue a lot. But your marriage is more of a convenience than a vibrant, growing relationship in the Lord Jesus Christ. God's glory is no longer its driving force. If you're honest, you ask, "Is there hope for my marriage?" Of course there is. But you must be willing to pursue change. Our prayer is that this booklet will help you think more biblically in your marriage. But you must do more than think about these things; you must roll up your sleeves and do them.

God has blessed us as husband and wife with a wonderful marriage. We view this as God's gracious gift. Over the last decades, we have had opportunity to counsel many people in troubled marriages as well as to provide premarital counseling to scores of engaged couples. Throughout the years, we have become convinced that there are a number of important principles that well-meaning Christians are ignorant of or are not following through on that could improve their marriage. In this booklet, we want to tell you some of the basics that we share with couples in premarital counseling.

So welcome to our home. Relax and have a seat. We promise to be succinct and straightforward. We offer you ten guidelines for building a godly marriage.[1] The first four address marriage as it is oriented toward God while the last six address marriage as it is oriented toward your spouse.

1. Building on the Word of God

God has revealed His will for the sacred institution of marriage in the Scriptures. Who can tell us better how to have a healthy and holy marriage than the One who instituted it? A God-glorifying marriage is a *Word-based* marriage. Thus we must let the Bible be the final authority for holy matrimony. In the Scriptures God tells us how to think about marriage, on what foundation to build a godly marriage, the

---

1. For a more detailed treatment of this subject, see Joel R. Beeke and James A. La Belle, *Living in a Godly Marriage* (Grand Rapids: Reformation Heritage Books, 2016), which summarizes in a contemporary way twenty-nine Puritan books written on the subject of marriage.

duties to which marriage obligates us and how to perform them, what struggles to expect in marriage and how to address them, and how to persevere in a difficult marriage. In His Word, God has graciously revealed what marriage is, why He created it, how to enjoy it, and how to glorify Him in it. Thus, if your marriage is to glorify God, it must be founded upon Scripture as the word of truth. We get the most fulfillment in marriage when we follow God's rules. He fashioned it from all eternity. He created our bodies physically and emotionally for marriage.

This relationship between man and woman started so beautifully in the garden of Paradise. Adam was created on the sixth day. The animals didn't fill Adam's need for companionship, however, so God formed Eve from Adam's rib to be his companion. Adam recognized himself in Eve and rejoiced in this gift from the Creator (Gen. 2:21–25). Adam and Eve were blessed in their life as husband and wife as long as they followed God's commands. We don't know how long this pure joy lasted, but we know it wasn't long enough. Eve ventured beyond the guidelines God had drawn, having believed a lie. She was deceived into thinking that disobedience was the way to greater happiness; still laboring under this deception, she reached out to Adam to join her in eating forbidden fruit. He did, and the rest of the story is our sad, sordid human history (Gen. 3:1–14). No more could Adam and Eve or anyone else have a perfect marriage. Wives throughout history would bristle under the leadership of their husbands. Childbirth would become painful and even dangerous for them. The gardening Adam had so enjoyed would become arduous and tedious; he would toil and sweat, and thorns and thistles would choke the good plants. He would work the soil his whole life in order to eat, then at death his body would return to the earth from which it had been taken. It was a dark future (Gen. 3:16–19).

But God did not leave Adam and Eve in this dark and hopeless state. Rather, even before God pronounced His punishment on the disobedient couple, He offered the solution. Genesis 3:15 records that after cursing the serpent and relegating him to a life of crawling in the dirt, God said He would turn the heart of the woman and her seed against the serpent and his seed, setting the stage for a spiritual conflict that would rage down through time. In the end, the seed of the woman would triumph over the seed of the serpent. In the fullness of time, God sent His own Son into the world, born of a woman, to crush the serpent's head and deliver His people from all the power of the devil (Gal. 4:4). All this came at great cost to Christ as He suffered during His life on earth and especially at the end, when He was nailed to the cross and bore our sins. Yet He endured the cross and even despised the shame of it as He kept His eyes fixed on the joy that was set before Him (Heb. 12:2).

This way of suffering mingled with joy is woven into the fiber of the gospel. Without shedding of blood there can be no remission of sin (Heb. 9:22). Jesus had to suffer and die so sinners like you and me wouldn't have to pay for our sins forever in the fires of hell. Then He arose and offered eternal life to all who believe in Him alone for salvation (Rom. 3:21–28).

The way of suffering and joy is also woven into marriage. Marriage is a precious flower its Designer allowed us to take from Paradise into this sinful world. God offers us salvation through Jesus Christ by Spirit-worked repentance and faith. Only when we are in Christ, joined to Him by faith, are we ready to enter into marriage.

A marriage built on the rock of God's Word will be a *gospel-shaped* marriage. In Ephesians 5 the apostle Paul says that husbands are to love their wives as Christ loves the church and that wives are to show reverence and submission to their husbands as the church submits to Christ. As Christ loves His church, so the husband must love his wife absolutely (v. 25), purposefully (v. 26), realistically (v. 27), and sacrificially (vv. 28–29). As a sinner, a husband will fall short of the infinite reach of Christ's love. Yet the Savior's love for His bride is to be every husband's goal and pattern. And as the husband faithfully strives, by God's grace, to love in this way, it will draw out his wife's submission, which parallels the church's submission to Christ (vv. 22–24). She is not to submit to her husband in *anything* that conflicts with her submission to Christ (v. 22), but in *everything* that is in keeping with her submission to Christ, she submits to her husband as she submits to Christ (v. 24).

It is important to understand that the submission the Lord asks of a wife is not a matter of hierarchy but of *function*. God assigns the role of leadership to the husband not because he is better than his wife, but because God delegates this authority to him. The wife's submission is not a servile subjection but a free, voluntary, God-honoring submission. In this way the relationship of husband and wife reflects the covenant love between Christ and His church and is patterned after the gospel.

An important ground rule that God lays down in Ephesians 5 is that the husband is responsible for carrying out *his* duties, and the wife is responsible for carrying out *her* duties. In our inherent self-righteousness, we tend to see our spouse's faults and blame the weaknesses of our marriage on him or her. We are more ready to justify our own actions and to magnify what is wrong with what our spouse is doing. But God is saying, "You each do your jobs, and let Me take care of the results. Obey My guidelines and trust Me to bless you."

In a Word-based marriage, both spouses are called to put God first, each other second, and themselves third. When both spouses receive grace to do this intentionally on a consistent basis, their marriage will bring glory to God. God will honor those who honor Him (1 Sam. 2:30). Here is the key to happiness in marriage: "Blessed is every one that feareth the LORD; that walketh in his ways" (Ps. 128:1).

God's biblical design for marriage is totally contrary to the world's ideas, so don't try to blend them together. The world says, "Marriage is supposed to make *me* happy. I want my spouse to please *me*. I will stay in this marriage as long as *I* am happy, but when the joy is gone, I am gone." This is the essence of a *me*-driven, self-centered marriage. It's like walking in quicksand. Each spouse tries to keep from sinking, sometimes by dragging the other down to do so. The more they struggle, the deeper they sink. But when Jesus Christ reaches out His hand and pulls them out of the mire and sets their feet on the solid Rock, they begin to thrive together. A *gospel*-driven marriage begins with self-denial, putting God first and your partner second. The believer says, "I was a lost sinner; now I'm a saved sinner redeemed by the precious blood of Jesus. My spouse is too. I love God because He first loved me. He gave me my beloved spouse. I am so grateful to God for His gifts that I want to love and serve Jesus Christ and my spouse for my whole life. I have deeper joy from loving and serving God and my spouse than I ever did when I served myself."

Which type of marriage are you working for, a *me*-driven marriage or a *gospel*-driven marriage?

2. Cultivating Spiritual Fellowship

The deepest fellowship is one in which you share your life with a dear friend in the presence of the living God. A God-glorifying marriage will cultivate such friendship. It is remarkable how so few Christians actually enjoy spiritual intimacy with their spouses. We are not talking about having family devotions, though that is also foundational to a God-honoring marriage. We are talking about sharing your faith with each other. It is not unusual for a pastor to visit a mourning widow and ask, "Do you believe your husband was a child of God?" only to hear the response, "I think so, but actually I don't know because he never spoke about it. He read the Bible often, he went to church faithfully, he was a good example, but he never talked about anything of his inner, spiritual life with me." How sad! The most important thing in life is faith in Christ Jesus, so please share your spiritual struggles, your faith, and your hopes with your spouse.

Obviously, this requires that you both have a living faith in Christ. Christians ought to marry only in the Lord (1 Cor. 7:39). If you are both Christians, you ought to regularly talk together about your spiritual experiences. Share your spiritual concerns, frustrations and triumphs, your pilgrimage and your progress. Talk about how the Lord is working in your life by His Word and Spirit. Make it a regular practice to tell your spouse the truths God has been teaching you in your Bible reading. Read and discuss spiritually edifying books. Listen to the preached Word together and engage in profitable conversation about it. Speaking about the things of God and your own souls is essential to a healthy, God-honoring marriage.

The purpose of such spiritual fellowship is to provoke one another to love and good works. Husbands and wives should help each other onward to grow in conformity to Christ. This requires humble vulnerability and willingness to share particular struggles with sin. It also requires the humility to lovingly counsel a struggling spouse by the application of Scripture to a particular condition. Husbands and wives should encourage each other in the faithful worship of God in public, in private, and as a family. They should behave as fellow pilgrims and travelers walking hand in hand toward the Celestial City.

3. Praying Together

A God-glorifying marriage will be a praying marriage. Prayer forces the mind into sobriety and affects the heart with the presence and majesty of God. Therefore, make praying together a priority. We realize that praying out loud can be intimidating for some Christians, and we should be patient with each other in this. But there is nothing like spending time in prayer each day as a couple, offering thanksgiving together for the day's blessings and petitioning God for the grace needed for the morrow.

Establish a time of prayer together as a regular part of your daily schedule and zealously guard that time. Don't put off prayer if your spouse asks you to pray at another time than the one you agreed on. You will be amazed at how even five or ten minutes of daily prayer together will fan the flame of marital intimacy. *Many couples spend hours together engaged in worldly entertainments* only to see their passions cool toward each other. Such hours will erode marriage, while time spent together in prayer and the Word will increase love for each other.

Praying together will also maintain the fellowship with God that fortifies you against the troubles and trials of marriage. Many couples think their greatest security against future hardship is a bank account well stocked with money. But what if hardship has shattered something that money cannot buy? What if the loss is something that money cannot replace? Without minimizing the need for saving against future unknowns, your greatest security against hardships is in the Lord. He has the strength you need to face trials, the wisdom you need to navigate the stormy seas of life, and the grace you need to endure hardship and suffering. *Vibrant communion and fellowship with God will not prevent the trials of marriage but will do much toward preventing you from responding to them dishonorably.*

As God is the Maker of souls, of marriages, and of our affections, we should constantly pray that He will grow our love for the spouse that He has given us and enable us to express that love in our words and actions. God graciously gives what He commands, so we look to Him to grant us faith, understanding, direction, and the will to obey, with the result that we ourselves work at obedience in marriage (John 15:4–5; Phil. 2:13). We must pray that He will keep our hearts knit together, give us increasing satisfaction in each other, and help us delight in each other's smiles, affection, touch, companionship, service, and time. We must pray that anything that would impair, diminish, or withdraw our love from our spouses would be kept from us (Matt. 6:13).

4. Practicing Family Worship

A God-glorifying marriage places a high priority on domestic or family worship of God.[2] As a married couple, strive to see that true religion is established in your home so that you may have a "little church" in your house (Ps. 101:2; Rom. 16:5). You should begin even before there are children involved; it will be much harder to do afterward. Every God-fearing husband ought to say with Joshua, "As for me and my house, we will serve the LORD" (Josh. 24:15).

Set aside time each day for family worship. Ideally, worship should be conducted twice a day, in the morning and in the evening. That fits best with

---

2. Most of this section is drawn from Joel R. Beeke, *Family Worship* (Grand Rapids: Reformation Heritage Books, 2005). For further insights on family worship, use this book as well as James W. Alexander, *Thoughts on Family Worship* (Ligonier, Pa.: Soli Deo Gloria, 1990).

scriptural directions for worship; the Old Testament teaches that each day was to be sanctified by the offering of morning and evening sacrifices as well as morning and evening prayers, and the New Testament church followed the pattern of morning and evening prayers. But for some families, family worship is scarcely possible more than once a day, after the evening meal. Either way, this time must be carefully guarded. There will be many distractions and temptations to neglect family worship, so a husband and wife should encourage each other to be faithful and consistent in this duty.

According to Scripture, God should be served in family worship in the following three ways. First, families should serve Him *by daily reading and instruction from the Word of God*. Moses called the people of Israel to keep God's words in their hearts and to "teach them diligently unto [their] children" (Deut. 6:6–7). Moses wasn't suggesting a little talk but diligent conversation and instruction that flow from the burning heart of a parent. In such instruction we as parents must be plain in meaning, pure in doctrine, relevant in application, and affectionate in manner. We should foster family dialogue around God's Word by asking questions and encouraging our children to ask questions.[3]

---

3. For a helpful aid in this area, use the *Family Worship Bible Guide*, ed. Joel R. Beeke, Michael P. V. Barrett, Gerald M. Bilkes, and Paul M. Smalley (Grand Rapids: Reformation Heritage Books, 2017).

Second, in this worship we should offer *daily prayer before the throne of God*. In Jeremiah 10:25, the prophet says, "Pour out thy fury upon the heathen that know thee not, and upon the families that call not on thy name." In other words, those who do not know and acknowledge God and do not call on His name bring wrath on themselves and their families. If your family is to be the object of God's pleasure, then you must pray. Such prayers should be short, simple, and solemn. They should include adoration of God, confession of sin, petitions, and thanksgiving.

Third, family worship should include *singing the praise of God daily*. Psalm 118:15 says, "The voice of rejoicing and salvation is in the tabernacles of the righteous." This is a clear reference to singing. The sound of rejoicing and salvation should rise from families and homes on a daily basis. Sing doctrinally pure songs, especially the Psalms. And sing them with thoughtfulness (Ps. 47:7) and feeling (Ps. 103:1). Husbands should say, "As for me and my household, we will seek the Lord, worship Him, and pray to Him as a family. We will read His Word, replete with instructions, and reinforce its teachings in our family. We will sing His praises and glory in His name."

5. Loving Your Spouse

Without sincere, selfless love, a marriage cannot glorify God. A husband and wife are to love each other with a strong, fervent, and steadfast love and not with a love that waxes and wanes with the changing tides of beauty, dress, or riches or fluctuates with emotions and lusts. It must be a generous love that pours itself out between spouses in a variety of expressions, gestures, looks, and actions.

Marital love is so precious that we must set a hedge around it. We are to have eyes only for each other and no other. Our imaginations should meander only toward our precious one. If we feel ourselves tempted by thoughts of others, we should pray for strength to guard our hearts, and then redouble our efforts to pour love into our spouse.

Nowhere is the nature of such love more profoundly portrayed than in 1 Corinthians 13:4–7. Here the apostle instructs the Corinthian church to show love to one another in the exercise of spiritual gifts "unto edifying" (1 Cor. 14:26). If such love is to be shown to fellow believers in the church, how much more should it operate in our relationship with our spouse? Paul tells us, first, that love is long-suffering and not easily provoked. So when our spouse irritates or displeases us, true love will restrain our anger and resentment and express itself in enduring patience.

Second, Paul says, love is kind and selfless. It seeks the well-being of the spouse in all things. Self-sacrificial kindness is a critical part of marriage. We once read of a couple who had become bitter toward each other. The wife decided to divorce her husband. She hated him so much that she wanted to shock him with divorce papers. So she thought she would be unusually kind to him for a month so he would think things were improving. Then he would be truly hurt when served with divorce papers. Near the end of the month, however, the wife noticed a change. But it was in her—not in him! She had begun to like her husband more. In fact, she was falling in love with him all over again. *Her* kindness had brought out *his* kindness, and their relationship was restored. Such is the power of love and kindness.

Third, Paul says that such love is void of envy and conceit. It is not jealous of a spouse's talent or success but joyfully shares in it. Fourth, true love thinks the best possible thoughts about one's spouse while still being realistic. And fifth, love bears, believes, hopes, and endures all things. Such love endures difficult times in marriage while praying and hoping for healing and resolution. Happy is the marriage marked by such love!

As the foundation of marriage, love must undergird and drive all duties within marriage. Such love makes everything in marriage easy while its absence makes everything hard. When love is abundant in a marriage, each partner will strive to meet the other's needs, and when it is lacking, all other duties become no more than cold, lifeless acts. When love fills your heart, your feet, hands, and lips move easily in the service of your beloved, but where love is lacking, duties are either neglected or performed in a hypocritical, slothful, and careless manner.

Marital love must be exclusive. It must be superlative love. You must love your spouse more than anyone else in this life. Other friends may hold a high place in our lives, but when it comes to heart-felt love, spiritual fellowship, and quality time spent together, blessed is that couple whose lives are so balanced that, under God, each holds the highest position in the other's heart.

6. Developing Good Communication Skills

When you marry, you enter a covenant of companionship. Malachi 2:14 says, "The wife of thy youth" is "thy companion, and the wife of thy covenant." But healthy, God-honoring companionship cannot exist without good communication. As husband and wife, you must seek by God's grace to develop good ways of talking with each other.

Healthy communication also involves listening. Be a good sounding board when your spouse needs to talk. James gives good advice when he says, "Be swift to hear, slow to speak, slow to wrath" (James 1:19). Husband and wife should each be willing to hear what the other has to say. No one should feel pressured to respond or be provoked to anger. An unseasonable rebuke or outburst of resentment will cause your spouse to retreat into silence — or worse, to resort to dishonesty, telling you only what you want to hear, even if it is not true. Many times the only concern or need is to "get something off your chest." Martyn Lloyd-Jones once said that if we want to be of help to others as counselors, we must learn not to be shocked or repelled by anything we hear. Each partner in a marriage must open the way for communication, listening to the other without responding in haste or in anger. When a wife says, "Honey, I feel this way," her husband should not say, "Do this or that, and you will get over it." If he does, she will most likely say in response, "I didn't ask you to tell me what to do. I just wanted you to know how I felt." That doesn't mean a husband or wife never needs counsel. But often he or she just wants to know that the other is there for him or her. We all want a sense of connection, and that sense lies at the heart of the idea of marriage. At times this sense of connection may result in tears. When open communication is real, tears do not spell disaster, but they can help purge pain. At such times, the spouse should hold the other in his or her arms, listen attentively, and love unconditionally.

Another aspect of healthy communication in marriage is discussing major decisions together and waiting until you have unity before moving ahead. Any decision that involves a major change for your family's life, home, work, or church should be made only after talking together about it, praying together, and coming to agreement. Although the husband is the head of the household, a godly man should not—with rare exceptions—lead his family against his godly wife's desires.

Healthy communication also involves the ability to take criticism from a spouse or give it without offending the other. This can be done by what we call the "sandwich principle." You lay down a slice of bread, as it were, by saying something like, "You are wonderful and I appreciate you in so many ways." You then name some ways that especially please you. Then you lay down a slice of meat, saying, "But I am concerned about something. I feel like you don't seem to care about how my days go. You seldom ask me about them, or, when you do, you don't seem to listen to my answer." Then you put down the other slice of bread and say, "Don't get me wrong, I am not criticizing you as a person. I am just concerned about one particular thing. I love you very much, and you have so many wonderful qualities." When you do offer such carefully constructed criticism, your partner will be more inclined to eat your sandwich. This is not manipulation; it is disciplined thankfulness.

Paul is a great model for this in the Epistles when he criticizes his readers. For example, when he writes to the Corinthians, he lays down a slice of bread in the first epistle's opening verses in which he thanks God for them and for their God-given graces and gifts and then assures them that Christ will confirm His work in them until the end (1:4–9). Beginning in 1 Corinthians 1:10, he begins to raise seven criticisms—seven slices of meat—together with his advice and solutions that point them to Christ. Then he concludes his epistle by laying down another slice of bread, telling them that he longs to see them again and will come as soon as possible, and, in the meantime, they should greet one another with a holy kiss (16:5–20). Though this was an unusually heavy sandwich to eat because of its seven layers of meat, Paul follows similar approaches in many of his other epistles.

What happens too often when we criticize our spouse is that we accompany it with strong, negative feelings. We forget that "the wrath of man worketh not the righteousness of God" (James 1:20). We criticize without ever mentioning how many things we do appreciate about our spouse. We fail to be thankful to God for the many good things our spouse brings into our lives. If a husband comes to his wife and simply says, "You don't care about me or how my days go," she might respond by saying, "Wait a minute! Look at all the things I do for you—and, by the way, you don't seem to care so terribly much about how my days go, either." There is a vast difference between wise counsel and selfish airing of complaints. Let us share constructive counsel with humble gratitude.

7. Complimenting Your Spouse

The mouth is the heart's vent,[x] so if our hearts are filled with gratitude and love for our spouse, that will be expressed in verbal affirmation and encouragement. A God-glorifying marriage glows with endearing compliments. Think of how Christ and His church speak to each other in the Song of Solomon. Christ says to His church, "O thou fairest among women"; "my love"; "thou art all fair, my love"; "there is no spot in thee"; "thou hast ravished my heart, my sister, my spouse"; "how much better is thy love than wine"; "my garden, my sister, my spouse"; "thine eyes…have overcome me"; "my dove, my undefiled is but one"; "O love, for delights." And the church addresses Christ in like manner: "Thy love is better than wine"; "thou whom my soul loveth"; "my well-beloved"; "thou art fair, my beloved, yea, pleasant"; "I am sick [with] love"; "my beloved [is] the chiefest among ten thousand"; "he is altogether lovely." If marital love is to reflect the fervent love between Christ and His church, then our marriages must be bright with loving exchanges that powerfully enflame and affirm each other.

As a couple we have counseled married couples for decades, but we have seldom been asked to counsel a couple that compliments each other every day. Couples function differently, of course, in affirming each other, but it is critical that each partner feel treasured and appreciated.

In our marriage, we love to give each other compliments. There are daily compliments on some aspect of each other's physical appearance. But more importantly, we give compliments to each other on various aspects of personality and how much those aspects mean to us.

The opposite of complimenting is complaining. Such grumbling focuses on the negative, essentially saying, "I wish my wife looked different" or "I wish my husband acted differently." Behind it all is the pride that says, "I have the right to a certain kind of spouse or to a certain amount of sexual pleasure and gratification." You have no right to anything except judgment for your sins. It is amazing how good God is in giving us anything good at all! Some marriages may break the heart and wound the soul. But when you see that you are a hell-deserving sinner, surely you must also admit, "I am receiving better than what I deserve." And if you have a believer for a mate, no matter how imperfect, you have cause to bless God every day. Instead of filing mental complaints against your spouse, fill your mind with appreciation and gratitude. Seek to express that gratefulness by way of compliments. It will go a long way in strengthening your marriage and thereby glorify God.

8. Cultivating Physical Intimacy

Sexual love in marriage is like fire in a fireplace. If the fire breaks through the boundaries of the fireplace and ignites other parts of the house, it can destroy your property, kill your family, and end your life. Likewise, sex outside of its God-ordained boundaries destroys and kills. What the world considers sexual freedom is really bondage to death. As Proverbs 6:32 says: "Whoso committeth adultery with a woman lacketh understanding: he that doeth it destroyeth his own soul." But we do not want to have such a fear of fire that we could never again enjoy the dancing flames in a fireplace. A blazing hearth is warm and beautiful. Likewise, sex within marriage is a warm and beautiful way to be close to the one you love.[4]

The Creator has placed us under an obligation to love our spouses with our bodies as well as with our souls. Have you realized that God commands you to make love regularly with your spouse if it is physically possible? Obviously, medical problems can make this impossible, at least for a time, and sometimes permanently. But when health permits, regular sexual intimacy is the will of God for married couples (Gen. 2:24; 1 Cor. 7:3–5).

Someone might object, saying this makes sex a duty and not an act of love. It drains sexual intimacy of all romance and makes it mechanical. Our response is that duty does not exclude delight any more than obedience to the law excludes love. Love is the essence of the law, and true obedience to God means serving Him with gladness (Ps. 100:2).

So when we think about bedroom activities, we should remember that the gospel brings with it the law. The seventh commandment does not merely forbid adultery; by positive implication it requires "conjugal love, and cohabitation" among married couples, as the Westminster Larger Catechism (Q. 138) reminds us.[5]

---

4. See Joel R. Beeke, *Friends and Lovers: Cultivating Companionship and Intimacy in Marriage* (Adelphi, Md.: Cruciform, 2012).

5. *Westminster Confession of Faith* (Glasgow: Free Presbyterian Publications, 2003), 222.

The best sex springs from a relationship in which we honor each other throughout life. This implies that sex should never degrade or demean a spouse. While the Bible does not go into detail about what kinds of sexual activity are permissible, it does make clear that we should not engage in sex in a way that treats someone like a slave, an animal, or an object. Sex should always communicate honor to a person in a way that is appropriate to God's image-bearer. The Heidelberg Catechism (Q. 108) puts its finger on essential values of the Christian life, purity and holiness, when it says that the seventh commandment teaches us to detest all uncleanness and "live chastely and temperately, whether in holy wedlock or in single life."

We should also realize that the sexual experience of a woman is somewhat different from that of a man. A man is commonly aroused visually by the sight of his wife, whereas a woman is aroused by such things as tenderness, thoughtfulness, talking, touching, and time spent together. Men often want to move quickly toward a sexual climax while women move more gradually. These are generalizations, of course, for a husband's needs for emotional intimacy can be every bit as great as or even greater than his wife's, and a wife's physical desires for sex can be every bit as great as or even greater than her husband's. The point is that you should learn how your spouse operates and work together for mutual satisfaction.

One key to good sex is to remember that you and your spouse do not exist for self but for each other. "Use not liberty for an occasion to the flesh, but by love serve one another" (Gal. 5:13). Isn't that what the gospel teaches us through the example of Christ? He made Himself a servant and humbled Himself (Phil. 2:6–8). He did not come to be served but to serve, giving His life as a ransom for many (Mark 10:45). Christ is the model for husbands in loving their wives (Eph. 5:25). So husbands, before reaching for your wife, remember that you are called to give yourself up for her.

Sexually, this means touching her heart before you touch her body. This starts earlier in the day with your kindness and helpfulness to her so her heart is tender toward you when you go to bed. But it also means that you keep touching her heart while you touch her body. Speak words of love to her. Praise her. And touch her body in ways that please her. Learn what she likes. Patiently offer that to her. It might involve considerable kissing or a backrub before you reach something explicitly sexual. But it will give your wife more profound sexual satisfaction.

And wives, speak words of love to your husband before, during, and after lovemaking. Your husband probably needs this more than he lets on. Respond to his love and touch, but don't hesitate to initiate love-making yourself. That makes most husbands feel wanted and desirable. Learn what he likes sexually (you may have to draw it out of him), and offer it to him. It will give your husband more profound sexual satisfaction and a deeper appreciation for you.

9. Developing Friendship and Common Interests

Becoming and remaining each other's best friend in marriage is critical. Jesus says friendship involves sharing what is on one's mind and heart (John 15:15), just as God shared His intentions with His friend Abraham (Gen. 18:17–18). Richard Baxter (1615–1691) wrote this about marriage:

> It is a mercy to have a faithful friend, that loveth you entirely, and is as true to you as yourself, to whom you may open your mind and communicate your affairs, and who would be ready to strengthen you, and divide the cares of your affairs and family with you, and help you to bear your burdens, and comfort you in your sorrows, and be the daily companion of your life, and partaker of your joys and sorrows.[6]

When you marry you enter into a covenant of companionship, as we have seen from Malachi 2:14, which means, among other things, that you each promise to "faithfully assist the other in all things that belong to this life and a better."[7] One couple we

---

6. *The Christian Directory*, 2.1, dir. 9, in *The Practical Works of the Rev. Richard Baxter*, ed. William Orme (London: James Duncan, 1830), 4:30.

7. "Form for the Confirmation of Marriage," in *The Psalter* (Grand Rapids: Reformation Heritage Books, 2011), 156.

know uses the five Ts to remember what companionship involves: Time, Thought, Talk, Tenderness, and Touch.

You are not a friend to your spouse if you seldom spend time together. Gary Smalley spent three years interviewing more than thirty families, all of whom were happy. The families had diverse geographic, social, and economic circumstances. But all these relationships had two things in common. First, the husband and wife found ways to spend time together and to do a fair number of things together, so that they tried not to be apart from each other too much. Second, they loved camping.[8] Maybe the thought of campfires and sleeping under stars thrills you. Or maybe the daddy-long-legs in the camp bathroom are more than you can handle. The point is this: do things together.

Friendship cannot be warmed up by thirty seconds in the microwave either. So much today is instant, but friendship is not. It costs something. It costs you yourself, your commitment, and your vulnerability. There are no rush orders in friendship. It must be baked slowly, gently, and continually if we want the flavor we are looking for.

One aspect of sharing your minds and hearts is discussing major decisions together and waiting until

8. Gary Smalley, *Hidden Keys of the Loving, Lasting Marriage* (Grand Rapids: Zondervan, 1988), 325–26.

you have unity before moving ahead.[9] Any decision that significantly affects your time or money or that involves a major change for your family's life, home, work, or church should be made only after talking together about it, praying together, and coming to a point of unity. As William Gouge (1575–1653) said, "Though the man be as the head, yet is the woman as the heart."[10]

Sharing your joys means sharing activities that you both enjoy. Look for areas of common interest and invest time and resources in them. If your spouse enjoys something that is not your favorite activity, learn to enjoy it. Go along to an event, and even if you can't appreciate it, enjoy his or her enjoyment. The more your lives overlap, the closer your friendship will become.[11]

Various forms of "togetherness intimacy" can be developed in marriage through talking together, reading, walking, sharing a hobby, exercising, and playing games. The most important thing is to share the experience of worship, in church and at home, and anything that builds up faith and promotes your spiritual edification. Do allow for exceptions to this guideline, however. In our marriage, one of us loves gardening and one of us hates it, due in part to

---

9. Smalley, *Hidden Keys*, 328.

10. William Gouge, *Of Domestical Duties* (1622; repr., n.p.: Puritan Reprints, 2006), 194 (3.4).

11. Adapted from Beeke, *Friends and Lovers*, 19–32.

grass and tree pollen allergies. In such cases the one spouse must understand the other spouse's preference and be content to do that activity alone.

10. Developing Togetherness in Parenting

Though this booklet is about marriage rather than parenting, married couples who parent without togetherness will bring substantial disharmony into their marriage and fail to glorify God as they should. In marriage, the husband exercises headship in relation to his wife, but in parenting they must exercise joint leadership. It is critical that both spouses understand this and agree on how it should be done. One of the chief points of contention in troubled marriages is that one parent is more lenient (or more severe) than the other. Children soon learn to play one parent against the other. If one parent then operates independently, the other may soon feel marginalized, and disharmony will permeate the home.

As a couple, we have worked hard to avoid this problem. If either of us receives a request from our children and we aren't sure of our spouse's take on the matter, we have learned to ask, "Have you talked with Mom [or Dad] about this?" If the child's response is yes, we then ask, "And what did she [or he] say?" If the answer was no, we would then say, "I will talk with Mom [or Dad] about this, and we will get back to you with our decision."

One of our children said to us, "It is so frustrating to come to you about something because you always work as a team. Why don't you ever disagree with each other?" We took that as a great compliment! And when our children got older, we believe they grew to appreciate that Dad and Mom were always of one mind in whatever was decided.

So if you want a family home that has low levels of stress and tension, talk over your children's concerns and give them a biblical, God-glorifying answer that represents your mutual convictions and decisions. In those rare cases in which you as parents cannot agree on a decision, hold off on giving an answer and continue to work toward agreement. If after a time you still cannot come to agreement and both feel equally strong about the issue, the wife should surrender the matter to her husband, and he should implement the decision after considering all the circumstances. At that point, however, a wise husband may well defer to his wife's advice.

To promote togetherness in marriage, it is paramount that each parent makes certain that the children respect the other parent. Since in most marriages the mother spends more time with the children than the father, children may treat their mother with less respect—especially if they can get away with it. For the sake of both the marriage and the family, it is critical that the husband does not tolerate such disrespect and supports his wife and that the wife sees to it that her husband is respected and honored in the home.

Conclusion

The ten principles set forth in this booklet are by no means exhaustive. But we believe they are important marks of a God-glorifying marriage. Strive to put these things into practice, and we can assure you that your marriage will be the better for it.

Most of all, remember that Christ's loving relationship with His church is the model for marriage. When God sets His love on us, He never gives up. That love is not just a euphoric feeling that comes over us; it is *action* grounded in right thinking and pure motives. Even when we think our spouse doesn't deserve it, we must continue to show him or her gracious, Christlike love. When such love flows both ways in marriage, a couple is blessed indeed.

As in all matters of personal sanctification, growth as a married couple takes time, diligence, faith in God, love for Christ, the light of God's Word, the help of the Holy Spirit, and a lowly, contrite heart. It is not enough merely to read this booklet or even to begin putting these things into practice; you must also continually grow in these areas until the day when death bids you part from your spouse. One day you will stand before God and answer for how you treated your spouse. Will you give an account of the great privilege you had of representing to the world the covenant love between Christ and His church? Will you be found faithful in that day? Our hope and prayer is that this booklet, under God's blessing, will help you grow in covenant faithfulness to your spouse and thereby glorify God.